Monographic Journals of the Near East *Afroasiatic Linguistics* 2/3 (May 1975)

This paper is part of the
Proceedings
of the
Second North-American Conference on Semitic Linguistics
Santa Barbara, California
March 25-26, 1974

REFERENCE TO TIME, SPACE AND OTHER TYPES OF QUANTIFICATION IN THE CITY DIALECT OF GAZA

Aharon Barnea
Department of Near Eastern Studies
University of California, Berkeley

This is a sociolinguistic analysis of some very common ways in the dialect to refer to concepts of time and space on one hand, and other types of quantification on the other. Those concepts of time and space do not depend so much upon any one system within the grammar, as they do upon the ways of analyzing and reporting experiences which have become fixed in the language as integrated "fashions of speaking." Those fashions of speaking are shown here in relating major events of the past, to time - "when" and "duration," in reference to age, place, space, etc. Through some very interesting "loose" types of adverbial constructions we report and analyze the oblique, indirect, approximated and circumstantial manner by which reference is made to those concepts in the language.

TABLE OF CONTENTS

page

TABLE OF CONTENTS 1

1. INTRODUCTION 2

2. REFERENCE TO TIME 3
   - 2.1. Major events in the past 3
     - 2.1.1. The beginning of Islam 3
     - 2.1.2. British Mandate 4
     - 2.1.3. The war of 1967 4
   - 2.2. Reference to period of day/year 5
   - 2.3. Reference to age 5
   - 2.4. Approximate duration 6
   - 2.5. "Confusion" with "Numeric time" 7

3. REFERENCE TO PLACE 7

4. OTHER TYPES OF QUANTIFICATION 9

BIBLIOGRAPHY 10

1. INTRODUCTION

It has long since been established that concepts of "Time," "Space" and "Matter" are not given in substantially the same form by experience to all men, but depend upon the nature of the language, through the use of which those concepts have been developed. Concepts of "Time" and "Space" do not depend so much upon ANY ONE SYSTEM within the grammar, as upon the ways of analyzing and reporting experience which have become fixed in the language, as integrated "FASHIONS OF SPEAKING." What we are dealing with, while trying to analyze the way a certain language makes reference to those concepts, is, in fact, an analysis of an extended theory of DEIXIS. Deixis is the term given to those aspects of language whose interpretation is relative to the occasion of the utterance; to the time of the utterance and to times before and after the utterance; to the location of the speaker and the intended audience. Ours must be an extended theory of those elements of deixis, a theory which would take in several other aspects of the speaker's SPATIAL, TEMPORAL and SOCIAL ORIENTATION. We shall try to describe those "fashions of speaking" which cut across the typical grammatical classifications, so that such a "fashion" may include lexical, morphological, syntactic and otherwise systematically diverse means, coordinated in a certain frame of consistency. On the syntactic level reference to time and space has been usually analyzed, and properly so, in terms of adverbials and clause supplements; the kind of syntactic constructions that were described by M. Cowell in his Grammar of Syrian Arabic as "supplementation." Cowell has noted that "supplementation is a loose type of construction, often syntactically vague or unmarked, in some cases requiring no particular word order."[1] Our examples show that time adverbials, like place adverbials, have no particular connection with the verb, but in fact, modify, syntactically, the entire verb phrase and even the entire sentence. They can occur quite freely with various types of verb phrases, and can be optionally extended to various sorts of supplemented sentences, which, syntactically, play the role of an adverbial.

Benjamin Whorf has argued[2] that our own concepts of 'time,' 'space' and 'matter' are conditioned, in part, by the structure of a particular language. Setting out to investigate the Hopi language he was faced with the problem whether there are traceable affinities between cultural and behavioral norms, and large-scale linguistic patterns. We shall see that there are definitely many connections (not correlations) between cultural norms and linguistic patterns in reference to time and space in the city dialect of Gaza. The "fashions of speaking" that we shall be dealing with in this paper are primarily those collected in Gaza[3], but we would not be surprised to find similar fashions in many other Arabic dialects, especially in places where the social structure and the social system are similar to those of the five neighborhoods (*ḥārāt*) which constitute the City of Gaza.[4]

---

[1]Cowell. 1964. pp. 515-533.

[2]Wharf. 1939. pp. 134-59.

[3]The material was collected by me (and recorded) during my field research stay in Gaza in the summer of 1973. Some preliminary observations had been taken already in the summer of 1971, when I stayed in Gaza for six weeks.

[4]The five neighborhoods which constitute the City of Gaza are: *Šiǧāᶜiyya, zeitūn, tuffāḥ, daraǧ* and *rimāl*.

Many of the socio-linguistic phenomena that will be described in this paper might be considered as universals in a way, and we would like to stress at this point that we do not have any intention of discriminating Gaza for the sake of our forthcoming analysis. Our purpose is mainly to describe an existing socio-linguistic situation, and to show how the language reflects some standards of social behavior and the connections between those standards and the way reference is made to time and space through generally used "fashions of speaking."[5]

2. REFERENCE TO TIME

Many social investigations have been made with regard to the problem of spatial and temporal orientation and perception. Sorokin and Merton[6] have shown that the emergence of "mathematical time," for example, was due to definite social developments, mostly connected with urbanization and industrialization. Gaza is a society in which such social developments have not yet taken place in the city itself, but the society is in constant culture-contact with other societies where those developments did occur. A society with a similar social structure has been studied by N.S. Eisenstadt[7], who concluded that: "The spatial and temporal orientation of social activities, their definite ordering and continuity, are focused on the ultimate values of a given social structure. Any given social situation can impose the spatial and temporal orientation inherent in it only insofar as it is related to the ultimate values and identifications of the social system."[8]

2.1 MAJOR EVENTS IN THE PAST

One of the first striking "fashions of speaking" is the reference to major common events of the society when relating to "time when" (in the past) and/or to "time-duration"[9] - on a continuum extending from some point in the past to some point in the present.

2.1.1. For a religious Moslem a way to express 'from time immemorial' - 'since the creation of the world' would be to refer to the beginning of Islam:

(1) *hāda mən ʾauwal-əd-dinya, mən ʾAWWAL-əL-ʾISLĀM lahalwaget, mən YŌM MUḤAMMAD lahalwaget.*
'This is (so) from the beginning of the world, from the BEGINNING OF ISLAM to this time, from the DAY OF MUHAMMAD to this time.'

---

[5]We are well aware of the fact that the "fashions of speaking" that we shall describe in this paper might be "universals;" this fact does not interfere with our goal to describe a socio-linguistic situation. We are also aware of the fact that the kind of description and analysis we intend to present here must be restricted, in many cases, to speakers of a certain layer in the society, namely, the lower uneducated and even illiterate part of the city. It has to be admitted that many of our examples are not a common feature of all native speakers of the dialect. I have interviewed all kinds of native speakers and, naturally, the more educated people do not converse in the same manner as the illiterate or preliterate speakers.

[6]Sorokin. 1943.

[7]The society that has been studied by N.S. Eisenstadt is that of the Kurdish Jews in a neighborhood called"Yemin Moshe" in Jerusalem. This community emigrated to Israel some 15 years before the study was done. Their social system and structure is, in many respects, very similar to that of Gaza, although our investigation did not take into consideration the direct situation in the refugee camps (those who have emigrated to the area in 1948). We have dealt only with the original inhabitants of the City of Gaza (*ɣazazwe ʾaṣliyyīn*).

[8]Eisenstadt. 1949. p. 67.

[9]Based on the analysis in Leech. 1970

2.1.2. In Gaza reference is often made to time with regard to the British (and Ottoman, Turkish) occupation, the 1948 war and the Israeli occupation of 1967. Reference to these events can be made in a direct or an indirect manner:

DIRECT:

(2) *gabəl yaᶜni talātīn sana ᵓayyām* əL-ᵓINTIDĀB əLBARIṬĀNI.
'30 years ago, at the time of the BRITISH MANDATE.'

INDIRECT:

Q: When did you get married?

(3) *fi-l-inglīz, gabəl-əl-həǧra.*
(Literally:) 'In the English (people) before the immigration.'[10]

The plural noun - English men = *ᵓinglīz* - is used as a time adverbial. (The expression Həǧra - might have been created under Islamic influence; the Islamic connotation is obvious).

Similarly I encountered:

Q: Did you go to school?

(4) *zamān*, ᵓAYYĀM YĀFA.
'A long time ago, in THE DAYS OF JAFFA.'

where the name of a city (Jaffa) is used as a time adverbial. An interesting reference is made to the year 1936, in which there were many incidents and strikes. An old man who is unaware of his age knows to tell me:

(5) SANAT ᵓIḌRĀB əS-SITTA U-TALĀTĪN, *ᵓana kān ᶜomri xamastaᶜšar sana.*
'AT THE YEAR OF THE STRIKE OF 36, my age was 15 years.'

Notice that the expression - the strike of 1936 = *iḍrāb əs-sitta u-talātīn*- has lost its numeric temporal value, became a lexicalized reference item with regard to time, and therefore has to be annexed to the time adverb - 'year' = *sana* in order to make reference to time.

2.1.3. The war of 1967 is a major time event reference in the dialect. Many speakers are not aware of the time which has passed since the war, but they express numeric time before and after the war:

DIRECT:

Q: When did he leave?

(6) *gabl-*əL-ḤARB *əbxamse u-talātīn yōm.*
'35 days before THE WAR.'[11]

INDIRECT:

(7) *gabəl ma yəṣīr taṣārīḥ, baᶜəd* əD-DUXŪL.
'Before there were permits, after THE ENTRANCE.'

---

[10]In the modern dialect in Gaza the term *həǧra* refers, in regular everyday speech, only to the immigration of the refugees from Palestine in 1948.

[11]The expression - *əlḥarb* 'The war,' refers only to the war of 1967. (Although the area and its people went through many wars in the last few decades, the recent one is being referred to as "The war").

The nominal expression - 'The entrance' = *əd əd-duxūl* has also become a time adverbial. Notice the use of: *gabəl ma*+Verb, as in: *GABƏL MA YƏṢĪR taṣārīḥ*. This kind of construction is very common to describe time 'before' and 'after,' like the following examples:

(8) *gabəl/baᶜəd ma {xaššat / tudxul} (ᶜalēna) ʾisraʾīl.*
'Before/after Israel entered (on us).'

It is clear that the speaker's temporal orientation is focused not on "mathematical time," but rather on major events which are integrated in his cultural norms, and to a certain extent, in his social structure.[12]

2.2. REFERENCE TO PERIOD OF THE DAY/YEAR

Reference to time of day is highly approximated. Rather than referring to a certain hour in the day, reference is made with regard to the cultural norms of division according to the APPROXIMATE TIMES OF PRAYER and SUNRISE/SUNSET:

(9) *u-zay ma-tgūl əs-saᶜa ḥdaᶜaš ʾaw əḥdaᶜaš u-nuṣṣ gabəl* ṢALĀT ƏḌ-ḌUHUR *bišwayya...*'
'and as you say, at 11, 11:30 - a little while before the NOON-PRAYER...'

(10) *ma BIFŪĞ ƏN-NAHĀR ʾilla bikūn kəll šī nāğez.*
'DAY (light) IS not COMING UP yet where everything is already ready. (literally), i.e. everything is ready even before sunrise.'

(11) *biwazzᶜū gabəl əš-ŠAMƏS, maᶜa əṬLŪᶜ əš-ŠAMƏS.*
'They distribute it (the bread) before THE SUN, with SUNRISE.'

We have here another example of a noun - 'the sun' = *əš-šaməs* which is used as a time adverbial, analogical to "sunrise." (The infinitive status constructus - *əṭlūᶜ* 'rise' becomes redundant for the sake of making reference to the time: sunrise).

(12) *barūḥ ᶜal-bayyāra, bağīš ʾilla guddām əL-MAƔRƏB.*
'I go to the orchard, and come back only a short while before SUNSET.'

Reference to time of the year is made with regard to agricultural seasons rather than months:

(13) *u-ʾiğa wagtēš? - ʾIYYĀM ƏL-ḤAṢĪDA.*
'And when did he come? - in the DAYS OF THE HARVEST.'

(Notice the "wh" question for time/when = *wagtēš*. Literally = 'time what?')

2.3. REFERENCE TO AGE

Regular reference to age in terms of exact number of years is a property of the educated layer of society. A great number of illiterate or preliterate speakers (especially women) are not aware of their (or others') exact age, but since they still need to make reference to age, any time adverbial describing age, especially one containing a numeric element, would be attached to a whole set of "approximation particles."

In many instances reference to age is connected with major events at the time of birth, or at any other given time in the past, or with various life-stages:

(14) *ᶜomri ZAY tamanya u-xamsīn. ma-hu ʾana ʾIBN TURKIYYA yaᶜni.*

[12]This fact, I believe, is predominant in the dialect, and can be proved statistically, not only impressionistically.

'My age is (something) LIKE 58. (It is the case that) I am the SON OF TURKEY, that is.'

Similar to the use of *ʾinglīz* for 'the time of the British,' here *turkiyya* - the name of the country becomes a deictic time adverbial, meaning: 'at the time of the Turkish Empire.'

(15) *fi ʿindo* ZAY *tamantaʿšar* *HĒKED.*
'He is (has) (something) LIKE 18 (OR) SO.'

Q: How old are you?

(16) *waḷḷa,* *BĪǦI* *tamanīn sena.*
'By God, IT COMES TO (=approximately) 80 years.'

(17) *xamsa u-xamsīn* *TAGRĪBAN YAʿNI.*
'55 NEARLY (approximately), THAT IS.'

(18) *YAʿNI TAGRĪBAN* *tnēn u-ʿišrīn halgēt ʾaw ʿišrīn ʾaw* *HĒKED ʾIŠI YAʿNI.*
'THAT IS, NEARLY 22 now or 20 or SOMETHING LIKE THAT, THAT IS.'

(19) *yaʿni* *FĪ* *xamsa u-talātīn, sitta u-talātīn.*
'That is, THERE IS 35, 36.'

(20) *waḷḷa* *YIMKəN* *fī xamsa u-sittin, sittin, baʿrafəš waḷḷa,* *MUMKəN* *xamsa u-sittin.*
'By God, MAYBE there is 65, 60; I don't know, by God, maybe 65.'

Q: How old were they when they died?

(21) *mātu* *U-HUMMA SɣĀR.* *yaʿni* *HAṬṬŪL HĒKED.* *əlwaḥade* *BəDHA TĪǦI TIMŠI-* *mātat.*
'They died while BEING SMALL. That is, THIS HEIGHT (or) SO. One (fem.) WANTED TO COME TO WALK - she died. (i.e. she was ABOUT TO START WALKING when she died.'

(22) *huwwa ʿammi lammən ǧawwaz* *KUNT ʾANA BAGAF.*
'i.e. When my uncle got married, I WAS (ALREADY) STANDING.'

The last two examples show how reference to age is made in terms of the individual's physical development.

All those examples illustrate some "fashions of speaking" referring to age, when the speaker is unaware of numeric (exact) age, and what are the means by which the language, reflecting cultural norms, overcomes this kind of (for us) obstacle.[13]

2.4. APPROXIMATE DURATION

Unawareness of exact time is prominent also with reference to duration of time.[14] In this case too, one finds the whole set of "approximation particles" which have been described with reference to age. Talking about the pilgrimage to Mecca:

(23) *bugʿud* *ḤAWĀLE ZAY* *xamastaʿšar yōm. lāken fatret əs-safar hādi tataḥammal* *ZAY ḤARAKET* *ʾarbʿīn yōm.*

[13] P. Abboud has suggested to me that the fact that people in the Arab society do not refer to age in exact numeric elements is a matter of religious beliefs and traditions (to avoid "the bad eye").

[14] Again, it should be stressed that this kind of unawareness would apply mainly to a certain layer of society. (Namely, the uneducated and illiterate speakers).

'He stays APPROXIMATELY LIKE 15 days, but this period of the trip takes (something) LIKE A MOTION (procedure) of 40 days.'

The following example shows how diverse are the syntactic structures and word order of expressions referring to "time duration." The same speaker gave me:

Q: How long have you been married?

(24)a. *ʾili fi-s-sanaʾilli hayna xaššēna fīha talāte snīn.*
'I have, in this year that we have entered (in) it (her) 3 years.'

b. *talāte snīn billi xaššēna hayna fīha.*
'3 years in that which we have entered it.'

c. *əs-sana hāda billi xaššēna fīha talāta.*
'This year in which we have entered - three.'

The time duration element - '3 years' occurs in (a.) at the end of the sentence, in the beginning (b.) and again at the end (mentioning only the number - 3) in (c.).

2.5. "CONFUSION" WITH "NUMERIC TIME"

When reference is made to time in terms of "mathematical time," the numeric element, very often, loses its face value:

Q: When did people start to settle in Gaza?

(25)a. *min tamanttalaf sana. masalan, əl-γalāyīni ʾaṣlo min γazza. rāḥ ʿala yāfa ṣallo talattalaf sana fi yāfa.*
'Since 8,000 (!) YEARS. For example, Alghalayini went to Jaffa, and he has been in Jaffa for 3,000 (!) YEARS.'

b. *fa-hadōl əl-ǧamaʿa kullum muttaʿawwidīn min xaməstalaf sana yəgūlu luγa čal.*
'And those people, all of them, are used, since 5,000 YEARS (!) to say language "čal."' (i.e. they have always used the word "čal" (for: "gal")).

Loss of numeric face value may result in an expression denoting moment, *point* of time, or point on a continuum to refer to a *period* of time or a section on a continuum:

(26) *wə-s-sēʿa yaʿni ʿašara ʿašara u-nuṣṣ əs-sēʿa əḥdaʿaš - əbyaxudha.*
'And at, that is, 10, 10:30 at 11 o'clock - he takes her.'

For the speaker a POINT OF TIME is not an integrated element in his temporal orientation, and reference is made to a PERIOD of time by points which have lost their face value. Many speakers are aware of the fact that "mathematical time" is a foreign cultural system. (They still have to deal with it in their language, especially in connection with official departments of the government):

(27) *kān lāzem yīǧi fi tamanya tamāni. ʾilyom tisʿa billifranǧi.*
'He was supposed to come on 8/8 (the 8th of August). Today is the 9th in the "foreign" (calendar).'[15]

3. REFERENCE TO PLACE

In his "Perception of Time and Space in the Situation of Culture-Contact" N.S. Eisenstadt

[15]The expression *əfranǧi* - is usually used to refer to the European way of dressing (*lābes əfranǧi*).

has assumed that contraction of social space to a given geographical location leads to discontinuity of spatial (social) perception. How is this idea reflected in "fashions of speaking" in Gaza when making reference to elements of space or place?

The social structure of the city is centered very much around the family, the neighborhood and the town. Making reference to place outside these contracted spatial constituents, shows in fact, some very obvious spatial discontinuities.

Talking about traditions of wedding procedures (where, usually, the groom and the bride are from the same family or at least from the same neighborhood), one says:

(28) *u-fī biğību mən* BARRA, *yaᶜni mən tāni ḥāra.*
'And there are those who bring (the bride) from OUTSIDE, that is, from another neighborhood.'

An interesting reference to place is made in Gaza with regard to Israel:

(29) *huwwa byəštγəl* BARRA *fi-srāᵓīl.*
'He works OUTSIDE, in Israel.'

as well as:

(30) *huwwa byəštγəl* ĞUWWA *fi-srāᵓīl.*
'He works INSIDE, in Israel.'

the difference being that the reference to Israel as 'outside' is made by speakers who, usually, do not leave their immediate geographical location (therefore - discontinuity), whereas those who regularly work in Israeli towns or go there every so often (whether the town is close to Gaza or not) will refer to it as "inside," in the latter case Gaza being the "outside." One refugee who has been living in Gaza for the last 25 years tells me:

(31) *ᵓana min-əl-ğiya, hādi garība mən ᵓaškəlūn u-*LAĞAY ŠWWAY.
'I am from Algiyya [a name of a village], this is close to Ashkelon [the nearest Israeli town to Gaza] and A LITTLE BIT TOWARDS US.' (Literally: "coming towards us").

In this case the spacial orientation being that Gaza is the center.

When a dweller of Al-sigāᶜiyya (the biggest neighborhood in Gaza) goes downtown he says:

(32) *ᵓana rāyeḥ* FŌG *ələmdīna.*
'I am going UP (to) the city.'

This place adverbial - *fōg* 'up' reveals the speaker's concept about the relationship between his own neighborhood, and downtown; the neighborhood being a "lower class" social area.

Every place outside the contracted geographical, social space is regarded as very far away; thus reference to places outside Gaza can be used for describing superlatives of adverbs like - "long":

(33) *humma kānu ṣaffīn* ZAY MIN HINA WA-ᵓABᶜAD MƏN-ƏL-YARMŪK.
'They were lined up LIKE FROM HERE (UP TO) FARTHER AWAY THAN THE YARMUK.' (A river in southern Syria).

With reference to space, one finds an adverbial which is usually used for quantity of liquids, used for non-liquid measure:

(34) *ma fi ḥīlto wala šibər ᵓarḍ, ᵓilla* NIṬFET *talatmīt mitər... .*
'He does not have even a foot of ground [literally: a span of the hand = *šibər*], except *a drop of* 300 meter...'

4. OTHER TYPES OF QUANTIFICATION

As opposed to time reference, reference to quantification of MONEY is done in exact mathematical aggregates. In terms of cultural norms, monetary needs acquire for them a definite meaning in relation to temporal sequence. Talking about "bridal money" (indicating quatity) one says:

(35) *halgēt bīṣal* SIT-SABᶜETTALĀF *lēra* ᵓ*isrāᵓīli.*
'Now it gets to 6-7,000 I.L.'

Notice the qualifier of the word *lēra* = 'pound.' The *nisba* suffixed adjectives as in ᵓ*isrāᵓīli* can be used alone without being depended (on the surface) on the object it qualifies. In other words, the name of the country + a *nisba* suffix by itself may be used for referring to monetary system, as the following two examples show:

(36) *niḥki* BILəSRĀᵓĪLI ᵓ*aw* BIMAṢRI?
'Shall we talk in ISRAELI (money) or EGYPTIAN (money)?

Or:

(37) ᵓ*ana ətǧauwazet* FALASṬĪNI, *kānat əl-*ᶜ*imla rəxīṣa.*
'I got married (with) PALESTINIAN (money), the currency was cheap.'

In the last example we can see that changes that have occured in the monetary system in the area are also reflected in the "fashions of speaking."

(38) ᶜ*amnauwal*[16] *šarēt-lo talat kutub əb*ᵓ*alf u-mitēn lēra.*
'Last year I bought him 3 books for 1,200 Pounds.'

Two expressions that I have found do not make reference to money in terms of mathematical aggregates:

(39) *ḥagg əš-šay* and *ḥagg əl-gahwa*
'Tea value' 'Coffee value'

These terms refer to the amount of money that one has to spend when he invites guests to his home. Again, common social norms are traceable in linguistic patterns, not through the regular (for us) kind of reference, which is usually made to indicate quantity (of money, in this case).

There are, of course, many other types of quantification which have not been analyzed here, since we did not see in them particularly interesting phenomena, typical to our dialect. Like the reference made to money, and unlike time reference, they would be of the "mathematical" type. This type of orientation has become predominant for most of the other types of quantification, since the social situation in which it became eminent is already integrated, as in Standard Average European (SAE) societies, with the ultimate values of the social system.

---

[16]Notice the morphophonemics of this compound. It might have developed from the Literary Arabic genitive construction: ᶜ*ām-in* ᵓ*auwal-in* → ᶜ*amnauwal*, with the loss of the genitive ending only in the second part of the compound, and retaining the *-n-* (without the vowel) of the ending on the first element of the compound. One might also try to explain it as being developed from an expression containing the definite article, where the *-l-* became *-n-* (a phenomenon very well known in Arabic dialects at word final position: ᵓ*ismā*ᶜ*īl* → ᵓ*ismā*ᶜ*īn*), (*əl*)ᶜ*ām əl-*ᵓ*auwal* → ᶜ*āmnauwal*.

Dealing with reference to time and space on one hand, and other types of quantification like monetary system on the other, we have tried to show that there are some CONNECTIONS, but not correlations or diagnostic correspondence between cultural norms and linguistic patterns, which are, frequently, different from what we are used to in SAE.

BIBLIOGRAPHY

Bloch, Ariel and Grotzfeld, Heinz. 1964. *Damaszenisch Arabische Texte*. Wiesbaden.

Cowell, Mark W. 1964. *A Reference Grammar of Syrian Arabic*. Georgetown University Press. pp. 515-532.

Eisenstadt, Samuel N. 1949. 'The Perception of Time and Space in a Situation of Culture-Contact.' *Journal of the Royal Anthropological Institute*, 79. pp. 63-68.

Fillmore, Charles J. 1966. 'Deictic Categories in the Semantics of "come."' *Foundations of Language*, 2. pp. 219-227.

Hallowell, A.I. 1937 'The Temporal Orientation in Western Civilization and in Preliterate Society.' *American Anthropology*, 39.

Leech, Geoffery N. 1970. *Towards a Semantic Description of English*. Indiana University Press.

Piamenta, Moshe. 1966. *Studies in the Syntax of Palestinian Arabic*. The Israel Oriental Society. Jerusalem.

_______. 1968. *Dabber 'Aravit. An Introduction to the Spoken Arabic of Palestine*. Tel-Aviv.

Sorokin, P. 1943. *Sociocultural Causality, Space, Time*. Durham, N. Carolina: Duke University Press.

Whorf, Benjamin L. 1939. 'The Relation of Habitual Thought and Behavior to Language.' *Language, Thought and Reality*. M.I.T. Press. pp. 134-159.

This paper is part of the
Proceedings
of the
First North-American Conference on Semitic Linguistics
Santa Barbara, California
March 24-25, 1973

THE SURVIVAL OF OBSOLETE HEBREW WORDS IN IDIOMATIC EXPRESSIONS

Raphael Nir
Deptartment of Applied Linguistics

The Hebrew University
Jerusalem, Israel

Obsolete Hebrew (and Aramaic) words surviving in idiomatic expressions constitute a special category in Modern Hebrew lexicon. These words are no more used in free combinations. The comprehension of such obsolete words surviving in idioms only has been tested with native speakers of Israeli Hebrew who tended to identify their sense with the meaning of the whole idiom or with the specific semantic role they seem to play within the idiomatic context.

In every living language, which has even a short history, one encounters the phenomenon of words discarded from current usage. This phenomenon is related to the dynamics of each living language, which naturally looks for new ways of expression. These obsolete words are not necessarily archaic. There are many archaic words still in current use in many languages, whereas relatively new words may become obsolete after being used for a short period. The reasons for obsolescence of certain words in a language are manifold. In some cases, the word is discarded from use because it is closely linked with a specific context which is no longer in use, and so the word becomes redundant and useless. In other cases a certain word is defeated by a rival-word, a synonym, and thus, rejected by the users.

Besides this phenomenon of words dropping out of current usage, i.e., OBSOLETE words, there is another occurence on the semantic level, which one might call OBSOLETE MEANING. This is related to cases in which a word remains in current use, but changes its meaning in such a way that the new sense overthrows the old one. In other words, a complete shift of meaning occurs, and the old sense becomes obsolete and is often forgotten.

It should be stressed, that in these cases the semantic change is a TOTAL one, unlike changes which result in polysemy - when two (or more) senses of the same word prevail in current use. Although some of the scholars dealing with lexicology or semantics mention the two phenomena of obsolete words and obsolete meanings under the same heading ("obsolescence"), they should be differentiated. The first is of lexicographic nature whereas the second one is semantic in character.

It is irrelevant to speak about "absolute" obsolescence. The notion of obsolescence is always related to linguistic behavior in a specific period in the history of a language. Does this imply that the concept of obsolescence is meaningless from a synchronistic point of view? In other words, will a word - being defined as "obsolete" in relation to other phases in the history of the language, be considered as non-existant from a synchronistic aspect? M.A. Pei and F. Gaynor in their *Dictionary of Linguistics* define *obsolete* as "no longer in general, current use." This definition is deficient, as it is not clear what the exact meaning of the adjectives *general* and *current* is. However, it is clear from this definition and from similar ones which can be found in other dictionaries or text books that a word marked as "obsolete" does not have to be discarded TOTALLY from usage. It is sufficient that it does not occur in GENERAL discourse to be considered as obsolete. This is of great importance to the lexicographer, who compiles a synchronic dictionary. He will be bound to ask himself whether to enter a word which is scarcely used and whether to mark it as obsolete. For instance, if a certain word occurs once or twice in current literature, but is very rarely used in ordinary discourse - should it be considered as obsolescent or rather as belonging to a "high" stylistic level, to a literary one? And what about words which are not used at all in free compounds, but still occur in frozen idiomatic expressions? Certainly a lexicographer could not ignore the current existence of such words although they are not to be found any more in "general" use.

The above mentioned questions have special significance in so far as Modern Hebrew is concerned. For many Hebrew speakers, the mere idea of compiling a synchronic dictionary of Modern Hebrew might seem extremely daring and even inappropriate, as they consider Modern Hebrew as still being in a process of revival. To their opinion, archaic words which appear in ancient Hebrew sources are not to be considered "obsolete" even if they are not to be found in current use. In his *Introduction to the Lexicography of Modern Hebrew*, Prof. Goshen-Gottstein expresses the view that each Hebrew word which appears in ancient Hebrew sources potentially belongs to the vocabulary of Modern Hebrew, for even if it is not to be found in current use, it might well be revived in the near future.[1] One finds a strong emotional attitude towards the miracle of the revival of the Hebrew language in Israel, and so there prevails a deep resentment towards "erasing" ancient Hebrew words from the vocabulary of Modern Hebrew. Each Hebrew word is treated almost as a holy entity. Still, in the following discussion we shall use the term "obsolete" as applying to Hebrew words which are generally not to be found in free compounds in current Modern Hebrew.

A number of words considered "obsolete" in a certain phase of a language can be found in some idiomatic expressions. These "language fossils" are bound compounds which contain obsolete components, and they serve in spoken as well as in written discourse. Some English examples are: *to and FRO*, *SPICK and span*.[2] Before we look closely at this phenomenon as it reveals itself in Modern Hebrew, it is pertinent to suggest a definition of "idiomatic expression," (in Hebrew: *niv*).

Our main assumption is that any "idiom" possesses at least one of two qualities - "idiomacy" or "stability." We shall use these terms as suggested by Mel'chuk;[3] the degree of IDIOMACY of a

---

[1]M.H. Goshen-Gottstein, *Introduction to the Lexicography of Modern Hebrew*, Jerusalem and Tel Aviv, 1969, 41, 300.

[2]Other examples can be found in W.J. Ball's, A *Practical Guide to Colloquial Idiom*, London, 1961, (3rd imp.).

[3]J.A. Mel'chuk, "The Terms 'Stability' and 'Idiomacy'," *Foreign Developments in Machine Translation and Information Processing*, M.S. Joint Publications Research Service, no. 20, 1961, pp. 11-22, mimeo., trans. fr. Russ.

given combination is determined by the number of collocations in which one or more of its components may serve in the sense it has in the given combination (in the case of an idiom, in its "idiomatic sense"). The degree of idiomacy will be as high as 100% in the case in which one of the components serves in the given sense in one collocation only, as the word *spick* is in the English expression *spick and span*. Hence such a conception of "degree of idiomacy" concerns each component separately. If more than one of the components serves in a given compound in an "idiomatic" sense, the total degree of idiomacy of the expression will, of course, be higher. At this stage the question rises, as to how to assess accurately the degree of idiomacy of a given compound. To overcome this difficulty, Bar-Hillel[4] suggests using a mono-lingual synchronic dictionary of the language concerned as a criterion. A collocation will be considered "idiomatic" if none of its meanings given in the dictionary is synonymous enough with the meaning of at least one of its components. However, how would one determine the degree of idiomacy of an expression, if one of its components is not entered at all in a synchronic dictionary, or is marked as "obsolete"? In such a case, the relevant component serves in the given expression only after being discarded from free usage. Hence, such a word has "zero meaning" outside the idiom from a synchronistic point of view. Evidently, this kind of combination would possess a high degree of idiomacy.

Besides the quality of idiomacy, or in place of it, an idiom might possess another characteristic - "stability." This characteristic may serve as an alternative criterion, whereby to distinguish an idiom from a free compound. The degree of stability of a given combination is assessed according to the amount of certainty by which its complete structure can be predicted given a part of it. In the case of expressions containing an obsolete word one can predict with almost absolute certainty, the structure of the whole idiom, if only the obsolete word is given. Therefore, the degree of stability of such an expression will be extremely high. In a lower degree of stability, we shall find combinations whose "stable component" serves in several collocations. The more collocations in which the component is found to be used, the less stable the given expression will be. In the extreme case, the expression will be labeled as a "free compound." Hence, stability, likewise idiomacy, is theoretically a measurable quality.

Most idioms possess both idiomacy and stability, but it is sufficient that a given collocation has either high idiomacy or high stability to be marked as an idiom. The assessment of the "idiomacy threshold" or "threshold of stability" is arbitrary. In some cases, it might be difficult to decide whether a certain degree of idiomacy or stability suffices to have a given expression considered as an idiom. However, most idiomatic expressions which possess a high degree of idiomacy, that is to say that one of their compounds serves in its idiomatic sense only (or almost only) in the given collocation, also possess a high degree of stability. For if the number of combinations in which a certain word serves in a special meaning is very small, then it follows that it should be relatively easy to predict the structure of the combination, if given the specific component.

There are, however, stable compounds which possess a rather low degree of idiomacy. This group includes lexical SIMILES. In these compounds one finds an explicit morpheme to denote the similarity between two concepts. In these cases, it is impossible to point out any idiomatic use of one of the components. Nevertheless, these expressions have a high degree of stability, because their complete structure can easily be predicted if part of it is given. For example: *az ka ari* ('strong as a lion'), and *kesheleg de eshtakad* ('it is real as last year's snow'). Beside similes there are several other idioms which retain a high degree of stability, though they are not very "idiomatic," as: *lo hayu hadevarim me olam* ('these things never happened'), and *ke az ken atah* ('then as now').

Some scholars who looked for characteristics of idiomatic expressions point out a criterion which

[4] J. Bar-Hillel, *Language and Information*, (Selected Essays on their theory and application), Addison-Wesley, London-Jerusalem, 1964.

has not been mentioned so far. They claim that many idioms in languages like English are constucted in a "non-grammatical" way, i.e., their grammatical structure deviates from the accepted current standards. L. Pearsall-Smith points out the constant tension that prevails between the accepted grammatical rules and the grammatical construction of certain idioms.[5] Hockett even claims that the accumulation of grammatical deviations in idiomatic expressions might ultimately influence the "ordinary" grammatical system of a language.[6] There seem to exist quite a number of grammatically deviating idioms in the English language. However, this phenomenon is very restricted in the Hebrew language. There are very few Hebrew idioms, which are constructed in an archaic way deviating from the current grammatical standards (*yetser hara* 'evil inclination', *nekhba el hakelim* 'was timid'). It seems to us, therefore, that this characteristic cannot serve as a criterion for the identification of idiomatic expressions in so far as the Hebrew language is concerned.

Is it then possible to define a Hebrew idiom as a combination of words possessing either high idiomacy or high stability, or both of these characteristics? Looking at Hebrew collocations one cannot ignore a large group of combinations that satisfy the above mentioned conditions, and yet are not usually considered as "idioms." We refer to a group of collocations called "set-phrases" or "fixed phrases." These phrases are lexical units, semantically parallel to "compound words" in other languages (a word which is composed of two or more lexical units, the combination of which constitutes a single word whose meaning often deviates from the meanings of the components). In the case of compound words, there exists no problem of distinguishing them from idioms, as an idiom is by definition a COMBINATION of words, (i.e., morphemes separated from each other). In Hebrew, however, we find a great number of combinations that possess high idiomacy and/or stability, but no Hebrew speaker will mark them as *nivim* (idioms). The striking characteristic that distinguishes them from idioms is the fact that they denote one distinct concept, and can usually be replaced by a single word, either in Hebrew (a synonym), or in another language (translation). For instance: *beyt-sohar* ('prison') can be replaced by *kele*, *kneh-midah* meaning 'criterion', etc.[7] A set-phrase equals one "semantic unit" whereas an idiom has always some wider connotations; as a rule it cannot be replaced by a synonym without distorting its figurative meaning. Therefore it is so difficult to translate an idiom, whereas it is much easier to translate a set phrase. Most idioms, then, have some kind of "additional meaning," or "semantic margin" (often emotional), which is rather hard to convey through any replacement.

One should be aware of the fact, that by excluding set-phrases from the definition of idioms (i.e., "any combination of words that possesses a high degree of idiomacy or stability or both"), we have not solved the problem of exactly defining an idiom in a satisfactory way. The definition suggested for a set-phrase is rather vague, and we are bound to find many border-cases, in which it is very difficult to decide whether a given combination is a set phrase or an idiom. However, this kind of difficulty seems to be unavoidable when dealing with semantic concepts.

We now turn back to idiomatic expressions which contain at least one component which is an obsolete word in a certain developmental phase of the language. Obviously, these combinations enjoy a high degree of both idiomacy and stability. They are highly idiomatic, because the obsolete word has a "zero meaning" outside the given collocation; (in some exceptional cases, one can find another combination or two in which these words have survived). They are also very "stable," for if given the obsolete word, it is easy to predict the whole expression, because there is only one (or two) expressions in the whole language in which this component is to be found. These Hebrew idioms are used almost exclusively in literary style, whereas, in other languages one can find them in colloquial discourse as well. It is interesting to note, that some of the obsolete words preserved in

---

[5] L. Pearsall-Smith, *Words and Idioms*, London, 1943, (5th ed.), pp. 177-182.

[6] C.F. Hockett, *A Course in Modern Linguistics*, New York, 1958, pp. 303-304.

[7] Other examples are: *din-vekheshbon* ('report'), *rashey-teyvot* ('initials'), *ba-koakh* ('representative'), *derishat-shalom* ('greeting'), *pesak-din* ('verdict').

these idioms find their way to "pseudo-literary" usage. High school students in Israel tend to use obsolete words (preserved in idioms) in their compositions. Besides using these words in the idiomatic expressions, they sometimes use them as free compounds. In the latter case, these words are often used in a sense which is quite different from the original one. In other words, the obsolete words acquire new meanings in these contexts. If practice will show that some of the words will actually be revived, but will be used in a new sense, then we shall have a case of "obsolete meaning" instead of word-obsolescence.

The questions we asked ourselves were: what is the nature of the meaning attached to obsolete words, which in contemporary standard Hebrew are used in idiomatic expressions only? In what instances does the original meaning prevail, and in which circumstances are they used in a different sense? Because of methodological reasons we preferred to examine the passive understanding of these words rather than speculate on the meaning attached to them by the writer who uses them in writing. We found about 80 such obsolete words that are used in contemporary literature in idiomatic expressions only. From these, 40 were selected and given to 30 high school students in Jerusalem, who were asked to write their meanings. All students belonged to the age group 15-16. From the answers given in the open questionnaires, four alternative meanings for each word were selected. The closed test comprised 24 words (16 were found to be inadequate). One of the four alternatives was the "correct" answer, namely the original meaning of the word, which served as its current sense when the word was still used in free compounds. The words were: *kritut* 'divorcing', *she'at* 'disgust, *krukhiya* 'crane (bird)', *gazit* 'hewn stones', *aliya* 'fat tail, lobe', *tigar* 'quarrel', *marud* 'wretched', *lemish'i* 'clean', *almin* 'worlds', *orkha* 'path', *eshtonot* 'thoughts', *shines* 'gird', *pinka* 'dish, plate', *minan* 'from us', *medokha* 'mortar', *metsarim* 'borders', *garem* 'body', *dimos* 'acquittal', *kurtsa* 'lump of dough', *kik* 'castor-oil seed', *kharum* 'flat', *tezazit* 'squall', *kibar* 'coarse flour', *lezut* 'crookedness'.[8]

As we expected, the test proved to be a difficult one, if by "correct answers" we mean finding the original meanings of the obsolete words. After analyzing the answers of 273 students in two high schools in Jerusalem, we found that the average achievement was eight "correct" answers, i.e., about 30%. However, the questionnaire was not designed to serve as an achievement test. Our main purpose was to find out the lines along which the "idiomatic" obsolete words are interpreted. For this purpose, an item-analysis of the alternative answers chosen by the examinees was performed (besides the "correct" meaning of the word, three distractors were chosen from the answers given to the open-test).

There appeared to be a high correlation between the "transparency"[9] of the idiom, in which the word serves as a component, and the number of "correct" answers given to that particular item. Thus, when the original meaning of the obsolete word is clearly reflected in the idiomatic expression, the number of "correct" answers was relatively high, e.g. 90% of the examinees pointed out the correct meaning of the *she'at* ('disgust'). The reason for that is obviously because its idiomatic sense in the expresseion *she'at nefesh* is exactly identical with the meaning of the whole expression, i.e., "revulsion." On the other hand, a semantically "opaque" idiom is an obvious obstacle for discovering the original sense of the obsolete component. Thus, only about 3% indicated the original meaning of *lemish'i* ('clean'), as the meaning of the idiom *megulakh lemish'i* ('is clean-shaven'), and so the obsolete word can also mean "completely" (50%).

Another factor is the frequency in which a certain idiom is used. The higher the frequency of the idiom, the better is its meaning known, and the higher is the chance that the meaning of the obsolete word be deduced from the sense of the whole idiom. For example, less than 10% pointed out the

---

[8]In Hebrew print: כריתות, שאט, כרוכיה, גזית, אליה, תגר, מרוד, למשעי,
עלמין, אורחא, עשתונות, שנס, פנכה, מנן, מדוכה, מצרים, גרם, דימוס, קורצא,
קיק, חרום, תזזית, קבר, לזות

[9]By "transparency" of an idiom, we mean the facility by which the verbal meanings of its components can be deduced from its idiomatical meaning. S. Ullmann (1964) includes this kind of transparency in the category of "semantic motivation" (pp. 91-93).

"correct" meaning of the word *lezut* ('crookedness'), as the idiom *lezut sefatayim* ('slander') is a rather rare one, and apparently many of the students were not familiar with its meaning.

In some cases, however, even frequently occuring idioms are known to the students merely in FORM, but not necessarily in meaning. The idiom *pat kibar* ('coarse meal bread'), is fairly common, but seemingly only 50% knew its exact meaning or guessed it. Half of the examinees chose either "bread" or "dry" as the meaning of *kibar*.

The influence of the idiom's meaning on the interpretation of the obsolete word, which serves as one of its components, is revealed in two directions:

1) by ascribing the meaning of the ENTIRE idiom to the meaning of the obsolete word,
2) by identifying the IDIOMATIC meaning of the word with its original sense.

The first trend is found, for instance, when the subjects of the experiment attributed the meaning 'prepared himself' to the word *shines*, whereas its original sense is 'girded a belt' (the entire idiom *shines motnav* meaning 'prepared himself'). Seemingly, those who chose this alternative didn't ask themselves wherefore should one add the word *motnav*, ('his hips'), if the whole sense of the idiom is already implied in the other component - *shines*. A similar instance is the word *kik*, which denotes the seed of the castor-oil plant. This word serves only in the idiom *shemen kik* ('castor-oil'), so about 50% of the examinees chose the sense "oil-medicament," transferring the meaning of the idiom to one of its components. In this way of interpretation, the obsolete word is grasped as an elliptical expression, as if one can delete the other components of the idiom, while the obsolete word "absorbs" the meaning of the entire combination.[10]

In other cases the meaning ascribed to the obsolete word is the idiomatic sense, i.e., the special sense in which the word functions in the idiomatic expression, as distinct from its original meaning. About 60% of the students chose the meaning 'tombs' for the word *almin* ('worlds' in Aramaic). Obviously, they paralleled the idiom *bet almin* to the other expression denoting 'cemetery' in Modern Hebrew, i.e., *bet kevarot*, ascribing the meaning of *kvarot* ('tombs') to the word *almin*. Only 23% chose the original meaning ('worlds'), in spite of the similarity between *almin* and *olamot* (the second word having the same meaning in Modern Hebrew as the Aramaic word *almin*). Likewise about 60% of the examinees chose the meaning 'self-control' for the word *eshtonot* whereas only 15% chose the original meaning ('thoughts'). The reason obviously lies in the meaning of the only idiom where this word is to be found, nowadays- *ibed et eshtonotav* ('lost his self-control'). In other words, the idiom is grasped as an ordinary collocation whose meaning can be derived from the combined meanings of its components. The tendency to ascribe the IDIOMATIC meaning to the separate obsolete word is noticeable in about 50% of the cases.[11]

Paradoxically, in some instances it seems, that the better the idioms are known, the greater is the subject's deviation from the original meaning of the obsolete word. For instance, 20% of the lower grade students chose the "correct" meaning for the word *medokha* ('mortar'), whereas none of the seniors chose it. Probably, more high-grade students knew the meaning of the idiom *yashav al hamedokha*, ('pondered'), and thus, more students took the idiomatic meaning of the obsolete word for its original sense. Indeed, in this case, if one does not happen to know the original meaning, it is impossible to derive it from the meaning of the idiom.

Obsolete Hebrew words surviving in idiomatic expressions constitute special category in Modern Hebrew vocabulary. They are not totally obsolete in the sense that they disappeared altogether from usage; however, these words are not used any more, or very rarely used, in free compounds. That may be a temporal state, and eventually these words may be used again in free compounds whether in their original sense or in their idiomatic one, i.e., in the sense conveyed to them by

---

[10]The phenomenon of ascribing the meaning of the whole expression to one of its components is rather common; cf., the word *sa'ad* acquired the meaning of the idiom *sa'ad libo* ('ate'), its original meaning being 'supported'.

[11]Some other instances are: *dimos*, *alya*, *pinka*, *medokha*, *metsarim*.

the idiom in which they still function. We counted about eighty such words, mainly nouns and adjectives.

As these words still serve in some stable compounds, their semantic status is a complex one. Usually the word is strongly associated with the idiomatic expression, and so Modern Hebrew speakers tend to identify its sense either with the meaning of the whole idiom or with its idiomatic meaning, i.e., with the semantic part it plays within the idiomatic context. If there happens to be a discrepancy between the word's original sense and its idiomatic meaning, Hebrew speakers will - as a rule - prefer the idiomatic one, unless the idiom concerned is unknown to them (either because it is used infrequently or because of its "semantic opaqueness").

If the word itself is "transparent" and its original sense deviates from its idiomatic meaning, we shall find that the more familiar the speaker is with the meaning of the idiom the less he would stick to the original meaning of the obsolete word. In a sense, acquaintance with the idiom may interfere with the "correct" interpretation of the obsolete component. One might assume, that in reverse cases, where the original meaning of the word is known and the precise meaning of the idiom unknown, the original meaning is assigned to the idiomatic one. However, these cases are rather rare as far as real obsolete words are concerned.

REFERENCES

J. Bar-Hillel, *Language and Information* (selected essays on their theory and application), Addison-Wesley, London & Jerusalem, 1964.

M.H. Goshen-Gottstein, *Introduction to the Lexicography of Modern Hebrew*, Schocken Publishing House, Jerusalem & Tel-Aviv, 1969, ##41,300.

C.F. Hockett, *A Course in Modern Linguistics*, Macmillan, New York, 1958.

J.A. Mel'chuk, "The terms 'stability' and 'idiomacy'", in: *Foreign Developments in Machine Translation and Information Processing*, M.S. joint Publication Research Service no. 20, 1961, pp. 11-12, mimeo. (translated from Russian).

L. Pearsall-Smith, *Words and Idioms*, Constable & Co., London 1943 (5th ed.), pp. 177-182.

S. Ullmann, *Semantics - an Introduction to the Science of Meaning*, Oxford, Basil Blackwell, 1964.

FIRST NORTH-AMERICAN CONFERENCE ON SEMITIC LINGUISTICS

Santa Barbara, California
March 24-25, 1973

The first North-American Conference on Semitic Linguistics was organized by Robert Hetzron (University of California, Santa Barbara) with the cooperation of Giorgio Buccellati (University of California, Los Angeles) and Joseph L. Malone (Barnard College--Columbia University). The purpose of the Conference is to promote the interest of Semitists in the various modern currents of linguistics. The full list of the papers presented at the 1973 Conference is given below. Those papers which have been submitted and accepted for inclusion in *AAL*, like the present one, are being published within the framework of the journal.

A. *Semitic and its Afroasiatic Cousins*

1. Carleton T. Hodge (University of Indiana), *The Nominal Sentence in Semitic* (=*AAL* 2/4).
2. G. Janssens (University of Ghent, Belgium), *The Semitic Verbal System* (=*AAL* 2/4).
3. J. B. Callender (UCLA), *Afroasiatic Cases and the Formation of Ancient Egyptian Verbal Constructions with Possessive Suffixes* (=*AAL* 2/6).
4. Russell G. Schuh (UCLA), *The Chadic Verbal System and its Afroasiatic Nature* (forthcoming in *AAL*).
5. Andrzej Zaborski (University of Cracow, Poland), *The Semitic External Plural in an Afroasiatic Perspective* (forthcoming in *AAL*).

B. *Ancient Semitic Languages*

6. Giorgio Buccellati (UCLA), *On the Akkadian "Attributive" Genitive* (forthcoming in *AAL*).
7. Daniel Ronnie Cohen (Columbia University), *Subject and Object in Biblical Aramaic: A Functional Approach Based on Form-Content Analysis* (=*AAL* 2/1).
8. Richard Steiner (Touro College, N.Y.), *Evidence from a Conditioned Sound Change for Lateral ḏ in Pre-Aramaic.*
9. Stanislav Segert (UCLA), *Verbal Categories of Some Northwest Semitic Languages: A Didactical Approach* (=*AAL* 2/5).
10. Charles Krahmalkov (University of Michigan), *On the Noun with Heavy Suffixes in Punic.*

C. *Hebrew*

11. Joseph L. Malone (Barnard College--Columbia University), *Systematic vs. Autonomous Phonemics and the Hebrew Grapheme "dagesh"* (=*AAL* 2/7).
12. Allan D. Corré (University of Wisconsin, Milwaukee), *"Wāw" and "Digamma"* (forthcoming in *AAL*).
13. Harvey Minkoff (Hunter College, N.Y.), *A Feature Analysis of the Development of Hebrew Cursive Scripts* (=*AAL* 1/7).
14. Raphael Nir (Hebrew University, Jerusalem), *The Survival of Obsolete Hebrew Words in Idiomatic Expressions* (=*AAL* 2/3).
15. Talmy Givón (UCLA), *On the Role of Perceptual Clues in Hebrew Relativization* (=*AAL* 2/8).
16. Alan C. Harris (UCLA), *The Relativization "which that is" in Israeli Hebrew.*

D. *Arabic*

17. Ariel A. Bloch (University of California, Berkeley), *Direct and Indirect Relative Clauses in Arabic.*
18. Frederic J. Cadora (Ohio State University), *Some Features of the Development of Telescoped Words in Arabic Dialects and the Status of Koiné II.*

E. *Ethiopian*

19. Gene B. Gragg (University of Chicago), *Morpheme Structure Conditions and Underlying Form in Amharic* (forthcoming in *AAL*).
20. C. Douglas Johnson (University of California, Santa Barbara), *Phonological Channels in Chaha* (=*AAL* 2/2).
21. Robert Hetzron (University of California, Santa Barbara), *The t-Converb in Western Gurage and the Role of Analogy in Historical Morphology* (=*AAL* 2/2).

F. *Beyond Afroasiatic*

22. Gilbert B. Davidowitz (New York), *Cognate Afroasiatic and Indoeuropean Affixes: Conjugational Person-Markers.*

SECOND NORTH–AMERICAN CONFERENCE ON SEMITIC LINGUISTICS

Santa Barbara, California
March 25-26, 1974

The second North-American Conference on Semitic Linguistics was held in Santa Barbara, in conjunction with the annual meeting of the American Oriental Society, on March 25-26, 1974. It was organized by Gene Gragg (University of Chicago), with Robert Hetzron being in charge of local arrangements. The full list of the papers presented at the 1974 Conference is given below; those papers which have been submitted and accepted for inclusion in *AAL*, like the present one, are being published within the framework of the journal.

A. Hebrew

1. Richard Steiner (Touro College, N.Y.), *On the Origin of the* heder ∿ h^{a}dar *Alternation in Hebrew.*
2. Talmy Givón (UCLA), *Verb Complements and Relative Clauses: A Diachronic Case Study in Biblical Hebrew* (=*AAL* 1/4).
3. Jack Zeldis (California State University, Fresno), *Bevakaša: A Study of Complementation in Modern Hebrew.*
4. Alan Harris (UCLA), *The Number Two / Collapsing: Two Problems in a Synchronic Description of Modern Hebrew.*

B. Aramaic

5. Yona Sabar (UCLA), *The Impact of Israeli Hebrew on the Neo-Aramaic Dialect of the Jews of Zacho in Israel.*

C. General Semitic

6. Alan Corré (University of Wisconsin, Milwaukee), *The Suprasegmental Feature of Length in Semitic* (forthcoming in *AAL*).

D. Arabic

7. Ariel Bloch (University of California, Berkeley), *Pronoun Externalization in Arabic.*
8. Aharon Barnea (University of California, Berkeley), *Reference to Time, Space and Other Types of Quantification in the City Dialect of Gaza* (=*AAL* 2/3).
9. Robert Hetzron (University of California, Santa Barbara), *Origin of Case-Government in Arabic Numerals.*

E. Ethiopic

10. Gene Gragg (University of Chicago), *Remarks on the Development of the Broken Plural System in Northern Ethiopic Semitic.*

AFROASIATIC LINGUISTICS

Volume One

1. P. Newman and R. G. Schuh, *The Hausa Aspect System*, 38 pp.
2. J. L. Malone, *The Development of the Anomalous Syriac Verb* eškāḥ *'To Find': A Case of Convergent Factors in Linguistic Change,* 10 pp.
3. R. Hetzron, *Extrinsic Ordering in Classical Arabic,* 25 pp.
4. T. Givón, *Verb Complements and Relative Clauses: A Diachronic Case Study in Biblical Hebrew,* 22 pp.
5. T. M. Johnstone, *The Modern South Arabian Languages,* 29 pp.
6. B. W. Andrzejewski, *Indicator Particles in Somali,* 69 pp.
7. H. Minkoff, *Graphemics and Diachrony: Some Evidence from Hebrew Cursive,* 16 pp.

Volume Two

1. D. R. Cohen, *Subject and Object in Biblical Aramaic: A Functional Approach Based on Form-Content Analysis,* 23 pp.
2. C. D. Johnson, *Phonological Channels in Chaha,* 13 pp.
   R. Hetzron, *The t-Converb in Western Gurage (The Role of Analogy in Historical Morphology),* 12 pp.
3. A. Barnea, *Reference to Time, Space and Other Types of Quantification in the City Dialect of Gaza,* 10 pp.
   R. Nir, *The Survival of Obsolete Hebrew Words in Idiomatic Expressions,* 7 pp.
4. C. T. Hodge, *The Nominal Sentence in Semitic*.
   G. Janssens, *The Semitic Verbal Tense System*.
5. S. Segert, *Verbal Categories of some Northwest Semitic Languages: A Didactical Approach.*
6. J. B. Callender, *Afroasiatic Cases and the Formation of Ancient Egyptian Constructions with Possessive Suffixes.*
7. J. L. Malone, *Systematic vs. Autonomous Phonemics and the Hebrew Grapheme* Dagesh.
8. T. Givón, *On the Role of Perceptual Clues in Hebrew Relativization.*
9. G. Buccellati, *On the Akkadian "Attributive" Genitive*.

Descriptive flyers
with complete lists of abstracts,
available on request.

undena publications

bibliotheca mesopotamica

Primary sources and interpretive analyses for the study of Mesopotamian civilization.

Volume 1. *Old Sumerian and Old Akkadian Texts in Philadelphia chiefly from Nippur.*
Part One: Literary and Lexical Texts and the Earliest Administrative Documents from Nippur.
By AAGE WESTENHOLZ. xii-210 pp., 3 plates. $18.50 (cloth), $12 (paper).

---

assur

A journal for the study of Assyrian as a dialect of Akkadian and of Assyria as a special aspect of Mesopotamian civilization.

Editors: K.H. DELLER, P. GARELLI, C. SAPORETTI. Subscription $12.50.
Volume 1 includes articles by S. Parpola, C. Saporetti, M. Fales, K. Grayson.

---

afroasiatic linguistics

A journal devoted to theoretical articles using Afroasiatic material, and to descriptive, historical and comparative studies.

Editor: R. HETZRON. Subscription $12.50.
The first two volumes include articles by P. Newman and R. Schuh, J.L. Malone, B.W. Andrzejewski, T. Givón, T.M. Johnstone, S. Segert, C.T. Hodge, D.R. Cohen, R. Nir, H. Minkoff.

---

afroasiatic dialects

A series of grammars providing concise descriptions of individual languages within the Afroasiatic family, and directed to scholars and students in the given language areas as well as in linguistics.

Editors: W. LESLAU and T.G. PENCHOEN.
Volume 1 (Berber). *Tamazight of the Ayt Ndhir.*
By T.G. PENCHOEN. 124 pp. $8.50.

---

sources and monographs on the ancient near east

Shorter fascicles making available original documents in English translation and important studies by modern scholars in the field of history, religion, literature, art and archaeology of the Ancient Near East.

Editor: G. BUCCELLATI. Subscription $10.
The first two volumes include fascicles by A. Falkenstein, B. Landsberger, I.M. Diakonoff, F.R. Kraus, R.I. Caplice, M. Cohen.

---

other volumes

Approaches to the Study of the Ancient Near East. A Volume of Studies offered to I.J. Gelb.
A collection of 27 articles on current trends and on the potential of new approaches in linguistic, literary, archaeological and historical fields. Edited by G. BUCCELLATI. 338 pp., 2 pl. (=Orientalia NS, Vol. 42, 1-2). $12.50.

A Bibliography of Homeric Scholarship. Preliminary Editio
By DAVID W. PACKARD and TANIA MEYERS. vi-184
Almost 4000 titles, listed alphabetically with a topical i tegories.

Professional and institutional discount of 20% on single copies
All prices are postpaid. Descriptive flyers and information on desk copies available on request.

Undena Publications, P.O. Box 97, Malibu, California 90265, U.S.A.